Shutting

关

Lu Piao

陆飘

Translated by Ouyang Yu

译者：欧阳昱

PUNCHER & WATTMANN

First published in 2020
Published by Puncher and Wattmann
PO Box 279
Waratah NSW 2298

http://www.puncherandwattmann.com
puncherandwattmann@bigpond.com

NATIONAL
LIBRARY
OF AUSTRALIA

A catalogue entry for this book is available from the National Library of
Australia.

ISBN   9781925780826

Printed by Lightning Source International

Contents

30 poems by Lu Piao, translated into English by Ouyang Yu

Born in Shanghai, in November, 1953, Lu Piao, whose original name is Lu Jinchang, is a member of the Shanghai Writers' Association and editor-in-chief of Pujiang Literature, and has published a number of poetry books, including A Dark River, Snow in the North, A Yellow Lamp through the Moon and Footsteps of a Thunder.

密林

密密的密林深处
密不透
风

透风了
不透风的墙千窗
百孔
叶翻红浪
秘密的
花
开了

水汩汩
低处流淌
初开的
苞
一放再
放

A Dense Forest

In the depths of a dense forest
So wind
Proof

That the wind leaked through
The wind-proof wall with thousands of windows
And hundreds of holes
The leaves were red waves
Where the secret
Flowers
Opened

The water, gurgling
Flowed to the lower places
Prompting the newly opened
Bud
To open and keep
Opening

耗

半夜
忘了关机
太阳还没出来
已耗尽了电

昨天坐出租车
司机说
那些吸冰的男女
混在屋子里不穿衣裤
穿衣裤的他反倒不自然

他们吸了之后
用橄榄油做润滑剂
激战时
上面在通话 下面在充电
一头在充
一头在耗——

那些毒东西
充电快耗电更快
几小时下来
就什么都
掏空
了

Consumption

I forgot to turn off my mobile phone
at midnight
its battery flat
even before the sunrise

the previous night when I took a cab
the cab driver said
the men and women who took ice
mixed with each other, naked, in a room
and those who had clothes on didn't feel at ease

after they took it
they used olive oil as lubricants
in a fierce fight
talking over the phone, up above, and charging, down below
charging at one end
and consuming it, at the other...

the toxic stuff
charging and discharging at a faster speed
powered out
in just
a few
hours

玉米棒

坚挺的玉米棒
插在黑夜里
鬃毛熊熊在燃烧

玉米地里
伸出一双脏手
撕下一层层包皮

那个赤裸的大汉　用力掰下
另一种阳具——

狞笑着
直直指向黑夜的
老洞！

The Corn Cob

The corn cob, erect
thrust into the dark night
its mane a roaring fire

in the cornfield
holding out a dirty hand
to strip layers of its foreskin

the naked man was forcibly breaking off
the male organ, of another kind—

and, with a dirty smile
he pointed it directly into the old hole
of the dark night

拍核桃

啪啦一声
核桃在玻璃桌面碎裂
一只寒鸟 从冰面惊起
在我头顶扑棱了一下 直冲云
霄——

妈呀 我哪来这么大的力量
可以打碎一个世界?
真真切切 一个世界被毁
现场一片惨烈——
一个最初的世界 混沌未开
一切尽在

要是一个二个拍下去
拍到最后会是什么结局?
我不敢再拍 只想把拍碎的世界重
合——

只合了一半——
轰然一下 冲上云霄的寒鸟
突然坠落——
冰面炸裂 眼前尽是伤心的碎片!

To Crack a Walnut

The walnut cracked open
On the glass-top table, with a crash

As a cold bird took flight in surprise, from the ice
Fluttering above my head and soaring into the clouds—

Oh, My! How could I possibly have had such strength
To smash a whole world?

But this is for real   a world destroyed
In a horrifying scene—

A pristine world
Retaining everything pre-chaos

What if I cracked one after another
What purpose would I achieve?

Afraid of doing it again, I
Tried to put the smashed world together—

Managing only half of it—
Before the cold bird that had soared into the cloud
Fell with
A sudden crash—

Splintering the ice
Filling my eyes with heart-breaking fragments

黑

浅黑淡黑浓黑
深黑
黑

黑发黑眼黑披风
黑马黑枪
白手
套

黑石黑草
黑水
三千里黑风
　七千里黑发
三响黑枪
砰砰
砰——

黑星坠落
黑山倒
下
黑狐逃了

空里流霜
只有
白鸦在
飞——

Black

Shallow black, pale black, dark black
Deep black
Black

Black hair, black eyes, black cape
Black horse, black gun
White hand
Glove

Black stone, black grass
Black water
Black wind for three thousand miles
　　Black hair for seven thousand miles
Three reports of black gun shots
Bang, bang
Bang –

A black star drops
A black mountain fa
lls
A black fox runs away

Frost flows in the air
Only
A white crow
Is flying –

雨

下雨落雨斜雨
风雨雷雨
云雨
阴雨淫雨梅雨
樱雨

春雨秋雨夏雨冬雨
冷雨寒雨韩雨
冻雨

大雨小雨粗雨细
雨
暴雨骤雨剑雨星雨
阵头雨毛毛雨及时雨

苦雨酸雨甘雨心雨
旧雨新雨
雨雨雨

红雨火雨太阳雨
血雨
黑雨白雨蓝雨
绿雨

有雨没雨求雨
晨雨夜雨
山雨

Rain

Raindown, raindrop, rainslanting
Windrain, thunderrain
Cloudrain
Yinrain, obscenerain, plumrain
Cherryrain

Springrain, autumnrain, summerrain, winterrain
Coldrain, chillrain, Korearain
Freezerain

Bigrain, smallrain, thickrain, thin
Rain
Violentrain, rushrain, swordrain, starrain
Showerrain, hairhairrain, timelyrain

Bitterrain, sourrain, sweetrain, heartrain
Oldrain, newrain
Rainrainrain

Redrain, firerain, sunrain
Bloodrain
Blackrain, whiterain, bluerain
Greenrain

Haverain, norain, seekrain
Morningrain, nightrain
Mountainrain

只给半小时

青藏高原
只给
半
小时

母亲
只
给半小
时

狼
藏棕熊
渡鸦
只
给
半小时

刚生下
必须
半小时之内
站
起来

立刻
找到自己母亲
跟着
行走 500 公里
才算来到

那个神秘的
世界

青藏高原
只
给藏小羚羊
半小
时

Only Half an Hour Allowed

The Qinghai-Tibet Plateau
Allows only
Half
An hour

Mother
Allows
Only half
An hour

Wolves
Tibetan blue bears
Ravens
Only
Allow
Half an hour

Must
Stand
Up
Within half an hour
Straight after birth

And immediately
Find one's own mother
Follow her
Covering 500 kilometres
Before reaching

The mysterious
World

The Qinghai-Tibet Plateau
Only
Allows the small Tibetan antelope
Half
An hour

石叫

一头雄狮
压住一头母狮

母狮的身下
压着一块石头

两头狮子的动作
震动石头

石头忍不住
发出女人的尖叫

The Shriek of a Stone

A lion
Lay on top of a lioness

The lioness
Lay on top of a stone

The act of the lion and the lioness
Shook the stone so much

That the stone couldn't help
Shrieking in a woman's voice

草原

草原三千里
一千里草
一千里风
一千里牛羊

草原三千里
八百里风
一千五百里牛羊
七百里草

草原三千里
只有风吹
不见草低

The Grassland

The grassland is three thousand miles
One thousand miles of grass
One thousand miles of wind
One thousand miles of cattle and sheep

The grassland is three thousand miles
Eight hundred miles of wind
One thousand five hundred miles of cattle and sheep
Seven hundred miles of grass

The grassland is three thousand miles
No low grass seen
Only wind blowing

秃树

整枝的人
拉着树的残臂断肢走了

被整过的树
光秃秃肃立在寒风中
嗦缩发抖
脚下
满地长发短发

记忆中被整的
男女也是这个样子
头颈里
挂着白色的牌子
上面写着黑字打着红叉叉

狼嚎的北风
压不住声讨的涛声！

The Denuded Tree

The guy who pruned off the branches
Walked away with the broken limbs of the tree

The punished tree
Stood bare and solemn, in the cold wind
Shivering
The ground at its foot
Strewn with hair, long and short

In memory, men and women
Punished, were also like this
With white boards
Hanging from their necks
Written with black characters crossed off in red

The northern wind, howling like wolves
Could not overcome the waves of denouncement!

椿树

在我村上的
早稻田
有棵椿树
我爬过的那棵
摸过鸟蛋的
那棵

我没捣过那棵上面的老巢
那老鸨骂人
把天都骂黑了
我只在树上撒了一泡尿
拿了她家三只蛋
没碰她的
三小姐

那棵椿树老高
比村上春树还高
站在上面
听得见云中的波涛

村上春树
爬过关西的椿树
也摸过日本的鸟蛋
他从日蛋里孵
出的笨鸟
飞进了挪威的
森林

The Tree of Heaven

In the early rice paddy
Of my village
There was a tree of heaven
The one
I climbed upon
To reach for the bird eggs

I did not disturb the old nest
The old madam abused people
Till the day went dark
All I did was piss on the tree
And took three eggs from her
But I didn't
Touch her Miss Three

The tree was so tall
It was taller than Village Up Spring Tree[1]
For when you stood on it
You could hear the waves in the clouds

As he
Climbed onto the tree of heaven in Kansai
And groped the Japanese bird eggs
The silly birds he hatched
From the Japanese eggs
Flew into the Norwegian
Woods

1   Literally 村上春树, the Chinese name of the Japanese writer, Murakami
Haruki.

找人抽

我拿着鞭子，
找人抽。

我把鞭子交给一位老农：
抽我吧，老伯，
我偷过你家地里的黄瓜地瓜！

老伯笑笑，　把鞭子还给我：
偷就偷了，有几个男人没偷过？
我问：难道你老曾经也偷过？
老伯没有啃声，撩起手来抽我！

我说：抽吧，使劲抽！

我把鞭子交给一位老妇：
婆婆，婆婆，请你抽我！

她说：你不抢我不偷我，我为啥要抽你？
我说：偷过，偷过！
我在草堆里偷过你的女儿！

婆婆笑笑：偷过就偷过，
女人的身体迟早会被男人偷去！
我问：难道你的身体也被野男人偷过？

老妇一把夺过鞭子，
劈头盖脸狠抽了我三鞭。

我拿着鞭子，
四处找人，
再也没人敢抽我！

我爬上高坡，
对着天空的喊：

天啊，老爷！
我无法把鞭子交到你手上，
你用光芒抽我吧！
我曾经想偷你的太阳和月亮
把太阳与月亮的位置换一换，
因为这个世界颠倒了黑白！

Looking for Someone to Lash Me Up

I held a whip
Looking for someone to lash me up

I handed the whip over to an old peasant:
Lash me up, Old Uncle
I have stolen cucumber and sweet potatoes in your fields!

Old Uncle smiled and gave it back to me:
That's all right. All men steal. Who hasn't?
I said: Have you?
Old Uncle said nothing but he lifted his hand to slap me

I said: Slap me, slap me hard!

I handed the whip over to an old woman:
Old Auntie, Old Auntie, please lash me up!

She said: you've never stolen from me. Why would I whip you?
I said: I did, I did!
I stole your daughter in a haystack!

Old Auntie smiled and said: That's fine
A woman's body, sooner or later, will have to be stolen by a man
I said: Has your body also been stolen by a wild man, too?

The old lady snatched the whip off me
And whipped me three times across my face

I now look for someone everywhere
Whip in hand
But no one dares to whip me!

I climb up a high slope
And cry to the sky:

Oh, heavens!
I can't hand the whip over to you
Or else you could whip me up with your lights
I did once want to steal your sun and moon
And swap their positions
Because this world has confused black and white!

意外

两个游客
在旅途中相识后
住进了同一个房间

两支牙刷
在盥洗间里相遇了
插足在同一个玻璃杯
它们面对着面
交叉着腿——

游客出游去了

面对着面 交叉着腿的牙刷
在杯中窃窃私语

突然噩耗传来——
两位游客在漂流中溺水
他们死亡的姿态:
面对着面 交叉着腿

By Accident

Two tourists
After meeting on their way
Checked into the same hotel room

Two toothbrushes
Met in the washroom
Thrust in the same glass
Face to face
Their legs entwined –

The tourists went out on a tour

The brushes, face to face and their legs entwined
Were whispering to each other in the glass

Bad news suddenly came –
The two tourists drowned while rafting
Their position in death:
Face to face, and their legs entwined

衣服

脱在床上的
——

扔在地上的
——

晾在一边的
——

我问
哪是你的？
哪是我的？

她说
穿得进的　是你的
穿不进的　是我的！

——都这个样子了
还分什么你我！

The Clothes

That were taken off on the bed

—

That were thrown on the floor

—

That were left on the side

—

I said
Which ones are yours
And which ones are mine?

She said
Those that you can get in are yours
Those that you can't are mine!

—Why bother telling you from me
if things are in this state of things!

抓痒

骑着电动车的小姑娘
撩了一下裙子
抓了抓大腿上的痒

对过的开车人
瞟了一眼
心里头痒痒

突地——
一条黄狗横穿马路
他急打一把方向
撞到了树上

在一棵老树的根部
结结实实
抓了一把痒！

Scratching an Itchy Part

The girl riding an electric bike
Was lifting her skirt
To scratch an itchy part on her thigh

The driver across the road
Glanced at it
His heart turning itchy

Suddenly –
A yellow dog ran across the road
The man turned his wheel abruptly
And rode into a tree

At the root of an old tree
He got his itchy part
Soundly scratched

怪病

酒中的老同学说他有怪病
常在梦里与亡妻对话
把身边的现妻吓醒！

现妻说他有毛病
医生却查不出病因

有一次他在梦中与人搏斗
把妻子踢到床下

有几次踢空了
自己把自己踢到了地上

他被医院隔离了三天
发现了脑电波的活动异常

医生说医院成立了专案组
正在追踪和他类似的病人

我没告诉他
我也有这样的病

十几年前
在梦里踢伤了人
老婆不得不和我离婚

A Strange Condition

His old classmate, while drinking, said that he was suffering from a strange
condition
Often talking to his dead wife in his dreams
Waking his current wife up with a fright

His current wife said that he'd got a condition
But the doctor couldn't find out the cause

On one occasion, he was fighting with someone in a dream
And kicked his wife off the bed

On several other occasions, he kicked at nothing
And ended up kicking himself onto the floor

After he was isolated in a hospital
Abnormal activities were found in his brainwaves

According to a doctor, the hospital had set up a case team
In pursuance of patients similar to him

I did not tell him that
I was also suffering from the same condition

As, more than a decade ago
My kickings in a dream had caused injuries to my wife
Who had to divorce me

奢侈一回

一个人飙沈海高速
一个人过杭州湾
一个人玩舟山群岛

一个人住一座山庄
一个人住总统套房
一个人躺两米大床

滚过来滚过去
想怎么睡就怎么睡
滚打了一辈子
还从来没有这样
滚打过

一个人用一个包房
一个人用八套餐具
一个人点十道大菜
一个人一饮三百杯

一个人吃喝
三个萌妹子陪
倒茶开瓶换碟拉窗帘
酒足菜饱
再上顶楼 KTV

奢侈一回吧
这样的奢侈 可以拉动
一个地方的
GDP

Enjoying Myself Alone, if Only for Once

Racing along the Shenyang-Hainan Island Freeway alone
Going across the Hangzhou Bay alone
Playing amidst the Zhoushan Archipelago alone

Staying in a mountain village alone
Occupying a presidential suite alone
Lying across a queen-size bed two metres wide, alone

Rolling this way and that
I could sleep whichever way I liked
I'd fought and rolled all my life
But had never done that
This way

Enjoying a private room alone
Using eight dinner sets alone
Ordering ten courses alone
Drinking three hundred glasses alone

Eating and drinking alone
Accompanied by three girls
Who poured tea for me, opened the bottles, replaced plates and pulled open the
                                                        curtains
And on a full stomach
I went to the KTV on the top floor

Just enjoying myself, if only for once
For such enjoyments could   pull off
The GDP
Of a place

火龙果

火龙果　七星剑
霸王花
三个不搭边的名字
偏偏是同一种
植物

就像陆飘　陆第
陆金昌
三个搭不上边的人
是同一个
我

霸王手持七星剑
与火龙
在空中格斗
火光烈焰之后
开花结果

结果
英雄的母亲怎样受孕的故事
在民间广泛传说

一个个龙鳞龙心红皮红心
红皮白心的故事
吃了之后
奇妙在我身上发生
他妈的
几十年的便秘没了

于是我吟唱
　我有果王
　以燕乐嘉宾之心

Fire Dragon Fruit

Fire-dragon fruit, Seven-star Sword
And Overlord Flower
Three unconnected names
Are in fact the same
Plant

Like Lu Piao   Lu Di
And Lu Jinchang
Three unconnected people
Are the same
I

The overlord, a seven-star sword in hand
Is fighting in the air
With the fire-dragon fruit
After the light of fire and burning flames
Flowers opened and fruit formed

As a result
The story of how the hero's mother got pregnant
Is spread far and wide in a legend

One after another, with dragon scales, dragon hearts, red skin and red hearts
In the story of red skins with white hearts
After I ate it
It worked wonders on me
Fuck
My constipation, lasting for decades, was gone

Thus I sing and chant:

I have got the king of fruit

To please the hearts of my guests

啃

她说
你都给了别人
只留给我
一把老
骨
头

他说
老骨头多好
又坚又
硬

她趴下
啃
用力
啃
那根包皮
骨
头

他在镜子里
看她
啃
直到那头
抬不
起
头

Gnawing

She said
You've given everything away
Leaving me only
The old
Bone
S

He said
The old bones are so good
They are firm
And hard

She got down on her knees
Gnawing
With an effort
Gnawing at
That
Bone-head, wrapped
In skin

He saw her
In the mirror
Gnawing
Till the head
Was unable
To raise
The head

山芋夫妻

窝在锅里的山芋，
揭了锅盖，满屋的香。

老夫在阳台看书，老妻
端着碗说：就挑出来几个
别的都出芽了！

老夫老妻在秋风里翻过山芋，
老夫刨碎过一只，
老妻心疼了半年。

老夫问老妻：
出了芽的山芋呢，
它们是怎么熬出头的？

老妻笑答：
有啥看头，
想想你当年，
是怎样被我从雪地里刨出来的。

The Potato Couple

The potatoes in the wok
Filled the house with an aroma, after the lid was lifted

The old husband was reading in the balcony and the old wife
Bowl in hand, said: I've only picked a few
The rest having all germinated

The husband and the wife had dug for potatoes in the autumn wind
When the husband broke one
He left the old wife feeling awful for six months

The husband asked the wife:
What about the germinating potatoes?
How did they manage to get to that stage?

The old wife smiled and said:
What are you talking about?
Don't you remember how
I dug you out of the snow in the old days?

早上敲门

咚咚咚——
我窝在沙发上看手机新闻
老婆在后阳台洗衣
她急忙去开门
踢到风扇电线差点摔倒——

居民组长催她去选举
关上门 她瞪了我一眼：
你没听见？
你去投票！

我站起身来说
我这个样子也能去？

她这才看见
我只穿
一件
红裤衩

Knocking in the Morning

Knock-knock, knock-knock —
Snuggling in the sofa, I was reading news on my mobile phone
And my wife was doing the laundry on the back balcony
When she went to answer the door
Nearly tripping over the cord of the electric fan —

The resident group leader urged her to go to the election
After closing the door behind her she stared at me:
Did you hear that?
You go and cast the vote!

I stood up and said:
Can I go like this?

It's not till then that she saw
I was wearing
Only
Red underpants

这座城市

这座城市
层层叠叠
叠向云头　叠向海边

这座城市
高层很高很高
最高的叠进天堂

这座城市
底层很低很低
最低的一层深入地狱

这座城市
是一个巨大的蚁巢
到处都在爬　到处都在啃
处处都可以钻进
钻出

这是一座混合叠加的城市
黄金和砖头　钢筋与骨头
美女和野兽——

白天的鲜花　夜里的垃圾
欢喜与眼泪
统统被抽水马桶
冲进阴沟

江水与股票

行情与海平面　一直在上涨！
而我的心
和这座城市　一直在下沉！

This City

This city
Overlapping
Towards the clouds   towards the sea

This city
Its top levels very, very high
The highest reaching paradise

This city
Its bottom levels very, very low
The lowest deep into hell

This city
Is a huge ant nest
Crawling everywhere   gnawing everywhere
Burrowing in and out
Of everywhere

This is a city of mixed overlappings
Gold and bricks   steel muscles and bones
Beauties and animals –

Flowers of the day   rubbish of the night
Pleasure and tears
All flushed into the sewage
By the toilets

River waters and shares

Market quotations and the sea level all rising!

And my heart

Has been sinking   with this city

接管

一根在墙上
一根在地下
两头
怎么对接?
徒弟说:
弄个弯头,套住两头,
就接上了!
老师傅说:
弯头太别扭,
干脆把下面的那根拔出来,
插进墙里——
直来直去
痛快!

Connecting the Tubes

One tube in the wall
Another underground
How to make the two ends
Meet?
The apprentice said:
Make an elbow to hook onto the ends
And they are connected!
The old master said:
The elbow is awkward
Just pull the lower one out
And stick it into the wall —
Straight in and straight out
It feels so great!

出入证

这个世界只有两道门
出门
入门
身份证　学生证　工作证
都是出入证

结婚证
也是出入证
花烛洞房的出入证
同进同出的
出入证

当然　也有许多无证的
只要有门
照样出的出
入的入

The Exit-Entry Permit

There are only two doors in the world
One for entry
And the other, for exit
ID cards, student cards, work cards
All exit-entry permits

Marriage certificates
Are also an exit-entry permit
To and from the bridal chamber lit with flowery candles
A permit
For mutual exit and entry

But, of course, there are many without that permit
As long as there are doors
They enter and exit
As usual

化武新闻

一群飞鸟
飞过叙利亚
鸟粪落在一部分武装分子
头上——

特朗普　特蕾莎　马克龙
认定是一次化武袭击
于是　三国合力
发射 JB 导弹——

好在巴沙尔早有准备
部署了普京的
S400
第二天他照常到总统府
上班

News about the Chemical Weapons

A flight of birds
Over Syria
Their droppings on the heads
Of a number of militarised elements –

Trump   Theresa   Macron
Deemed it an attack with chemical weapons
And the three countries   in a combined effort
Launched the JB missiles –

The good thing is that Bashar, well prepared
Had deployed Putin's
S400
The next day   he went to work as usual
In the presidential palace

绿色通缉令

九十年代
阳澄湖
一批先富起来的大闸蟹
横行湖上湖下
偷税逃税
遭到警方通缉

潜逃美国马里兰州的
大闸蟹
在水下地下定居
逐步泛滥到田园 城区
马里兰州警方

不得不
以危及其它种族
危及美利坚国家安全
为由 发出通缉令
通缉大批深绿色的
China 大闸
蟹

（注：有感于美马里兰州发"螃蟹通缉令"齐抓蟹）

The Green Notice

In the 1990s
The freshwater Dazha crabs in the Yangcheng Lake
That had got rich first
Were running amuck around the lake
Dodging and evading taxes
Till they were wanted by the police

The ones that had escaped to Maryland
In America
Took residence underground and under water
Till they went viral to the fields and the city districts
The Maryland police

Had to issue a green notice
To arrest large batches of dark-green
Great China
Crabs
As they endanger the security
Of other races
And the United States of America

(Note: this poem was inspired by a notice issued to catch the crabs in
Maryland)

吃花蛤

旁桌
吃没炒开的花蛤
用指甲
掰开

女人看不惯：
你掰掰掰
掰得人难受
看看你弄得满手油
酱酱
腻心死了

女儿插嘴：
老爸老是瞎掰
手多脏

我也点了花蛤
没开的就咬
破
用舌头
舔——

旁女人
嘀咕：
看人家多痛快
直接用
嘴——

Eating the Flower Clams

Someone next table
Was eating a stir-fried flower clam
Trying to pry it open
With his fingers

My woman didn't like that:
You pry, pry, pry
It's so insufferable
Look how oily you got your hands
With soy-sauce
So disgusting

My daughter interjected:
Dad always does it blindly
His hands so dirty

I also ordered the flower clams
I'd break the unopened ones
Open
And lick them
With my tongue −

The woman next table
Whispered:
See how much this person was enjoying himself
Directly using
His mouth −

打坐

别人练站
我练坐
别人练劈叉
我练盘
腿
别人练气功
我练弃功
别人练忘我
我练有我
别人排除杂念
我收集杂念
别人想最干净的事物
我想最肮脏的东西
别人练意
我练痰
把心里最肮脏的思想
把嘴里粘乎乎的唾沫
练成浓痰
再把浓痰炼成子弹
射
出去

Beat-sitting in Meditation

If others practice standing

I practice sitting

If they practice doing the splits

I practice crossing my

Legs

If they practice qigong

I practice giving it up

If they practice forgetting themselves

I practice having myself

If they exclude distracting thoughts

I collect them

If they think of the cleanest things

I think of the dirtiest things

If they practice minding

I practice spitting

Till the dirtiest thoughts in my heart

And the sticky phlegm in my mouth

Turn into thick phlegm

Then I'll practice turning the phlegm into a bullet

And shooting

It

等

她在等
约她的人约了别人

他从白色的车里出来
上了地铁

深夜
白色的车在细雨中
等人打开门

她在等
一夜虚掩着房门

Waiting

She's waiting
The one dating her was now dating someone else

He came out of a white car
And got onto the subway

Late at night
The white car in the fine rain
Was waiting for someone to open the door

She's waiting
Keeping her door ajar, all night

想发脾气

一匹马
跑进了一家咖啡店
吓跑了顾客——
那是一匹英式马？
还是意式法式马？
记不得了

记得少年时
我常惹事
砸那家的窗户
砸这家的水缸
没少欺负麦子油菜
叔叔说我
像一头骚牛，到处碰撞！

现在。我骚不动了
不过有时幻想当总统
当上某国总统
可以随便发脾气
发马脾气　牛脾气
也可发驴脾气
看谁不顺眼
就尥他
蹶子

Wanting to Throw Tantrums

A horse

Runs into a café

Scaring the customers away –

Is that an English horse

Or an Italian or French one?

Don't remember

All I can remember is that when I was a teenager

I'd often make trouble

Smashing this family's water vat

Or that family's window

Bullying the wheat and the rapeseed

Uncle chided me, saying:

You are like a horny bull, running wild everywhere!

Now, I'm no longer horny

Occasionally, though, I dream of becoming a president

And if I become one

I can throw tantrums at random

Horse tantrums and bull tantrums

Or even donkey tantrums

If I don't like someone

I can rear

And throw him

Off my back

中耳炎

洗头脏水
流进了左耳

夜里　脏水
从左耳流出
弄脏了枕头　床单

处男年纪
耳膜穿孔
左耳常常哭泣

医生说
耳膜可以修复——
可我　不想修复了
怕　再弄破

An Inflammation of the Middle Ear

The dirty water, after washing the head
flowed into the left ear

at night   the dirty water
flowed out of the left ear
dirtying the pillow   the sheets

at a virgin age, the man
had his eardrum pierced
his left ear often weeping

the doctor said
the eardrum can be repaired—
but I   don't want that done
for fear that   it might break open again

长脚蜘蛛

排卵期 她
有了
肚子慢慢大了

和谁 怎么有的
她不知道

那肚子 像袋子
包了
好几个

她用长脚旋转
卵袋
用丝扎紧

抱着肚子
等孩子们出生

出生后的子女们
没吃的
把她吃了

The long-legged spider

In the ovulatory period   she
got pregnant
her belly swelling up

with whom   and how
she had no idea

the belly   like a bag
wrapping up
a few more bags

her long legs were twisting about
and her egg pouch
tightly tied with silk

hugging her belly
she waited for the birth of her kids

who, having nothing to eat
after the birth
ate her up

折腾

你折腾我
我折腾你
自己折腾自己

结婚 离婚
折腾娘子
买房 卖房
折腾房子
入股 撤股
折腾票子
生了儿子
老子折腾小子
小子折腾老子

文人墨客也没少折腾
写诗的折腾文字
写字的折腾笔纸
画图的折腾颜料
蹲坑时还折腾草纸

折腾惯了
生了病还要折腾
折腾护士 折腾医生
于是 医生护士合伙折腾病人

官场在折腾
商场在折腾
职场在折腾

情场更是折腾

官场折腾出腐败
商场折腾出虚假
职场折腾出蟑螂
情场折腾出小三

折腾啊折腾
人生本来就是折腾

Zheteng

You zheteng me
I zheteng you
One zhetengs oneself

Marrying   divorcing
Mutually zhetenging
Buying properties   selling properties
Zhetening with properties
Buying shares   withdrawing shares
Zhetenging with bills
When a son is born
The old man zhetengs his little one
The little one zhetengs his old man

Men and women of letters are much into zhetenging, too
Poets zheteng their words
Calligraphers zheteng their paper and brushes
Painters zheteng their pigments
Shitters zheteng their toilet paper

Notwithstanding one's used to zhetenging
Falling ill is more zhetenging
You zheteng the nurses   you zheteng the doctors
As a result, the doctors and nurses collaborate to zheteng their patients

In bureaucratic circles there is zhetenging
In business circles there is zhetenging
In workplaces there is zhetenging

And, in love, more zhetenging

Till corruption is zhetenged out in the bureaucratic circles
Fraudulence in the business circles
Cockroaches in the workplaces
And Little Threes (concubines) in love

Zhetenging, ah, zhetenging
Life is all about zhetenging[2]

---

2 Although the Chinese expression, 'zheteng', has found its way into the Urban Dictionary, https://www.urbandictionary.com/define.php?term=Z-Turn, the explanation is far from satisfactory. With no English equivalents, the word （折腾） basically means turning things upside down, making a mess of things, and spending one's life doing meaningless things again and again.

冬虫夏草

花草间的蛾子
繁衍草原的后代——

他们的后代是虫
虫在土里 吃着草根——

死了的冬虫 站着
站着 直到头上长草——

紫色的草 白色的雪
五月的草原 流着眼泪

为你死 为你生
来生 还为你
做虫 做草!

The winter-insect-summer-grass

Moths among the flowers and the grass
Breeding the offspring of the grassland—

Their offspring is insects
Who, in the earth   eat the roots—

When dead, the winter insects   stand
Standing   till their heads are covered with grass—

The purple grass   the white snow
The grassland in May   is in tears

Dying for you   born for you
In the next life   remaining the insects   remaining the grass
For you alone!

白纸片

卷被风
卷起白纸片
飞了起来——

三片飘落地板
两片落入床与墙的夹缝
一片飞向圣经——

原来　白纸片像诗一样
有的会飞翔
有的会零落
有的追求信仰

一只白蝴蝶从圣经里飞出
飞进窗外的阳光—

Pieces of white paper

Turned up, by the wind
Turning up the pieces of white paper
Flying up—

Three pieces dropped drifting onto the floor
Two between the bed and the wall
One towards the Bible—

Right   the pieces of white paper, like poetry
Can fly
Can drop
Can pursue faith

A white butterfly flies out of the Bible
Into the sunshine outside the window—

骑

骑马有什么意思？
至多两只脚
换成了四只脚
骑自行车有什么意思？
至多两只脚
换成了两个轮子

要骑就骑宝马奔驰
不用鞭子
照样飞奔
要骑就骑老鹰
在鹰背上鸟瞰天下
要骑就骑嫦娥1号2号3号
几千年的梦想
几天就成真了

要么就骑牛
骑羊
骑猪骑鸭
骑鸡——
只图一时痛快！

Riding

What is the point of riding a horse?
It's just replacing two feet
With four
What is the point of riding a bike?
It's just replacing two feet
With two wheels

If one rides at all, one must ride a BMW or a Benz
Without whipping it
It'll gallop away
If one rides at all, one must ride an eagle
Overlooking the under-heaven on its back
If one rides at all, one must ride Chang E No. 1, No. 2 and No. 3
A dream of thousand years
Is realized in a few days

Or ride a cow
A sheep
A pig, a duck
Or a chick—
Just to get the sheer pleasure!

12 路

闵行 12 路——
起点：南辅路西环路
终点：浦连路召楼路

上海地铁 12——
起点：闵行七莘路
终点：浦东金海路

G12——
起点：上海
终点：北京

世界 12 路——
起点 -- 终点
不知道在
哪里？

Route 12

Route 12 to Minhang—
Starting at: Nanfu Road and Xihuan Road
Stopping at: Pulian Road and Zhaolou Road

Route 12, Shanghai Subway—
Starting at: Qixin Road, Minhang
Stopping at: Jinhai Road, Pudong

G12—
Starting in: Shanghai
Stopping in: Beijing

Route 12 the World—
Starting – Stopping
No one knows
Where they are

唤醒高俅

让他醒来
对他磕头
叫他祖宗
请他代表
中国足球
用头
用膝盖
用脚尖
颠球
把中国
颠进
世界杯

Waking Gao Qiu up[3]

To keep him awake
To kowtow to him
To call him an ancestor
To get him to represent
The Chinese soccer team
Popping and tipping the ball
With his head
His knees
His tiptoes
Taking China
Right into
The World Cup

---

3 Gao Qiu is a government official in the Song dynasty. See for more information here: https://en.wikipedia.org/wiki/Gao_Qiu

看图

一头乱发
卷起的狂风暴雨
把我掀起来
抛向半空
然后落下
砸碎海面——
在浪涛中挣扎
沉浮——
当我浮上来的
时候
你站在海边
泪流满面
满身湿
透

Looking at the map

The wild wind and storm rain, churned up
By a headful of disheveled hair
Lifted me up
Throwing me in mid-air
Before dropping me
Smashing into the sea—
Struggling in the waves
Sinking and floating—
When I
Emerged
You stood by the sea
In tears
Your whole person
Soaked through

鱼刺

吃夜饭
一根鲫鱼刺
塞了牙缝
用牙签
剔
用小指甲
抠
出了血
也没弄出来

后来
我用另一根鱼刺
刺它——
它不得不出来了

The fishbone

At dinner
A fishbone of a crucian carp
Got stuck between my teeth
I tried to get it out
With a toothpick
Then with the nail
Of my little finger
Till it bled
But it remained there

Subsequently, I had
To use another fishbone
To pierce at it—
It had to come out

狗领导

她到孤狗院
领养一只无主狗
训狗师问她是否养过狗？
她摇摇头

狗师告诉她秘诀：
养狗就是当狗领导
你自信脚步坚定
狗狗才肯跟你走——

狗师给她一根狗绳
让她走进狗圈
学会系狗
她小心给狗下套
牵着它跨过狗
门

她收紧绳子遛狗
狗趴在地上不肯走
狗师说：你的绳子勒痛了狗脖
把绳结转到脖下
让狗起抬头

她遵照指示
与狗同行
从容走过狗栅
全然不顾旁狗叫唤

初试及格
狗师再嘱咐：
用餐让它养成良好习惯：
先闻狗食
学会尊重食物

知道养狗之道了吗？
知道：
遵从狗性尊重狗权
学会与狗相处

The dog leader

She went to an orphanage of dogs
To adopt a masterless dog
When the trainer asked if she had kept a dog
She shook her head

The trainer told her a secret:
To keep a dog is to play the dog leader
If you are confident, walking in steady steps
The dog will follow you—

The trainer gave her a dog leash
And let her walk into the dog ring
To learn how to tie a dog
Carefully, she laid a loose
Led the dog through the dog
Door

When she tightened the leash to walk the dog
The dog lay on its stomach
The trainer said: your leash made the neck of the dog sore
But if you shift the knot underneath its neck
It'll raise its head

She followed the instructions
And walked side by side with the dog
Easily through the dog fence
Totally ignoring the barking of the other dogs

Thus passing the first test

When the trainer instructed again:

When you feed the dog you must have the dog form a good habit:

You must first smell the food

To let it learn to respect it

Know how to keep a dog?

I do:

Follow its nature and respect its rights

And learn to co-exist with it

回答

门外一个声音在叫喊:
爬出来吧,你想要什么?
狗夹着尾巴,
低着身子从小门出来。

一个声音在问:
看门,流浪,你想做什么?
看门有吃有喝,流浪享受自由!

狗回答:
要一套西服,一根领带!
那个声音问:
你要西服领带干吗?

答:
做你的随从!
那个声音说:为什么?

狗说:
想和你一样,
手上带着金戒,
卡里存着金钱
屋里养着金发!

那个声音冷笑:
不行, 绝对不行,
你不能做我的随从!

狗哭丧着脸质问：
为什么？你能行，我不行？

答复如下：
你穿着西服戴着领带，
走在大街上，夹在人群里，
改不了
那副人模狗样！

The reply

A voice was crying outside the door:
Crawl out. What do you want?
The dog, its tail between its legs
Lowering itself, came out of the tiny door

A voice was asking:
Which do you prefer, to guard the door or to wander around?
If you guard the door you are fed and if you wander around you have
freedom!

The dog replied:
I want suit and tie!
The voice said:
Why do you want that?

The reply:
I'll follow you!
The voice said: Why?

The dog said:
I want to be like you
Wearing a ring
Money in the bank
And a golden-haired one at home!

The voice said, with a sneer:
No, absolutely no
You can't act as my follower!

The dog, its face pulled, said:
But why? If you can, why can't I?

The reply:
If you wear suit and tie
Walk on the street, mixed with the people
You can't change
The doggy way you look!

钻被头洞

小时候
钻被窝叫钻被头洞
兄弟姐妹
在被头洞里
摸鱼

撕破里子是常有的事
撕破了干脆钻进夹层里面
与棉絮搅在一块
假亲热

摸鱼摸错地方
摸出大蒜头臭屁——
撕破面子
是常态
游戏过头吃麻栗子
也是常态

在野外
钻芦苇荡
钻草窝钻麦垛
是钻被头洞的另一路玩法
那样可以玩出一大片广阔天地

河浜里
钻被头洞更有意思
水被头没什么面子里子
怎么撕也撕不破

怎么钻都行——

闭着眼睛屏住呼吸
一口气狗扒泥
水底走泥丸
一猛子扎到 p 岸——
猛子越扎越浅
最后只好
爬上岸穿短裤回家

长大了
不再玩钻被头洞
而在被子里玩别的花样

Burrowing into the holes in the quilt

When I was little
Burrowing into a hole in the quilt was called *zuan beitou*
Us siblings were
Groping for fish
In the quilt holes

The lining would often get torn
In that case, we'd simply burrow into the interlinings
Mixing with the cotton batting
Pretending to be intimate

Groping fish would lead to wrong places
Smelling garlic farts—
Tearing face
Was common
    And it's not uncommon to get knocked on the head by the adult's knuckles
When it went too far

Outside in the fields
To burrow into the reeds
Or into the haystack, the rick
Was another way of quilt burrowing
A way that could create a vastness of heavens

In the creeks
Quilt-burrowing was even more interesting
The water quilt had no linings
And refused to be torn

However hard you burrowed in it—

Closing your eyes and holding your breath
You swam, dog-like
Crawling on the bottom, rolling the mud balls
And, in one sitting, got to the other bank—
The more you burrowed, the shallower you got
And you ended up
Going home, pulling up your shorts

When I grew up
I stopped burrowing into the quilt holes
Instead, I was into other kinds of playing in the quilt

床上的太阳

太阳从不升起
落下

升起落下的
是你我
我从床上升起 你
从床上
落下

你是云层
我撕破
你
我是高山
顶起
你

大地是一张蹦蹦床
让你蹦 让我跶
最后
让你我
躺下——

Sun in the bed

The sun never rises
Or falls

Those who rise and fall
Are you and I
I rise from the bed   you
Fall
From the bed

You are layers of cloud
I tear you
Apart
I am a tall mountain
Propping you
Up

The land is a trampoline
That allows you   and I, to jump
Putting
You and I
To a final rest—

我的伊甸

西山
与
东山
隔空相望

西山上神警告：
不可偷吃禁果！

东山里圣人曰：
所谓伊人，在水一方！

在东西之间
我来回
早攀西峰　夜宿东山
一会儿东
一会儿西

其实哪儿也没去
我只在房间里
偷吃禁果
君子好逑

My Eden

West Hill
Looks to
East Hill
Across the space

The deity on West Hill warns:
No eating the forbidden fruit!

The saint on Eastern Hill says:
The one after my own heart is on the other side of the river!

Between East and West
I come and go
Climbing West Hill in the morning   staying for the night on East Hill
Now East
Now West

In fact, I haven't been anywhere
I stay in my own room
Stealing a bite of the forbidden fruit
That a gentleman is desirous of

关

关窗
关门
关住春色
把绿把红关外面
把鸟关在天空

我不想招惹
那些香草花蝶
招惹飞禽
走狗

让众鸟在天空里
我的鸟
在自己的
山谷
里

我不想飞
不想扑
腾

做只呆鸟
孵
自个的
蛋

Shutting

Shut the window
Shut the door
Shut the colours of spring
Keep the green and the red shut outside
Keep the birds shut in the sky

I do not want to offend
The fragrant grass, the flowers, the butterflies
Nor do I want to offend
The flying fowl
And running dogs

Let the crowded birds stay in the sky
And let my bird
Stay
In my own
Valley

I do not want to fly
I do not want to
Flutter

All I want to do is be a silly bird
Hatching my
Own
Eggs

下锅

馄饨饺子
下一锅
北方的饺子
南方的馄饨
南方
北方
下在一锅

冰箱里
各过各的
热锅中
同锅共济
厚皮的薄皮的
荠菜的白菜的
捏紧的 包紧的
各自
心知肚知

出锅了
你拿你的碗
我抽我的筷子
你吃你的 我
夹我的

下锅 就是过日子
哪天我把馄饨饺子面条
下一锅

In the wok

Won ton and dumplings
A wok
Of northern dumplings
And southern won ton
The south
And the north
In one wok

In the fridge
They keep to themselves, separate
In the wok
They share the boat
Thick-skinned and thin-skinned
Stuffing of shepherd's purse and bok choy
Tightly pinched   or wrapped
Each knowing it
Clearly

When they are out of the wok
You take your bowl
I pick up my chopsticks
You eat yours   I
Pick up mine

Down in the wok   that is living
One of these days I'll put won ton, dumplings and noodles
In the same wok

老天的账本

大地高高低低，世界永远不平。
太阳给高山戴上皇冠，高山即可君临天下。
君令如山，山倒下来压死人，不倒下来吓死人。
山高一层碰着天，官大一级压死人。
不过，再高的山，再大的官，有天压着！

太阳每天巡视大地，地上的坏事都看在眼里记在账上。
老天的账本，藏在哪里谁也不知道。
或许藏在水底，或许藏在云中，或许藏在地底的裂缝。
暴风卷席的时刻，洪水滔天的时刻，大地裂开的时刻，
老天的账本就会翻开来——

The account-book of the old heavens

The land is uneven and the world is never flat.

The sun crowns the tall mountains, which lord it over the under-heaven.

The emperor's order is like a mountain. When it falls, the mountain crushes

people to death, or if not crushing them to death, it frightens them to death.

The mountain, if higher by one level, touches the sky, and the official, if

bigger by one level, crushes one to death.

Still, however high the mountain and however big the official, they are

overridden by heavens

The sun tours the earth daily, seeing everything bad and keeping it in its

account-book.

But where is the account-book of the old heavens hidden? No one knows.

Possibly under water or in the cloud, or in the crevices of the rock bottom.

When the storm is raised, the floor reaches the sky and the land cracks open

It will be opened—

装饰

衫木地板 柚木地板
复合地板
一间一间
一层一层——
大厅 卧室 阁楼 夹层

地砖 墙砖 文化砖
鹅卵石
厨房间 卫生间 化妆间
小花园
窗口

粉刷过的墙壁
再上涂料
立邦 多乐士 邦立 士乐多
刷平 刷刷平
平刷刷

中央空调安在
屋顶
调节冬夏
越调控
室内室外
温差越
大

Decoration

The floor of fir   of teak
The laminate floor
Room after room
Level after level—
A hall   a bedroom   an attic   the sandwich construction

Ground bricks   wall bricks   culture bricks
Pebbles
A kitchen   a toilet   a dressing room
A small garden
A window

Painted walls
Coated also
Nippon   Dulux   Bangli   Sileton
Painting plane   painting painting plane
Plane painting

The central heating installed
On the rooftop
To adjust the winter and the summer
The more it's adjusted
The greater
The temperature
Between indoors and outdoors

床单

阳台上
床单滴滴答答
滴着残梦的露水 ----

阳光射破云层
越飘越轻的床单
放着幻灯 ----

昨夜的月
在乡野的床上翻滚
浑身沾满了菜花 草青——

不知谁家的新娘
早早起来
偷偷洗了床单？

The bed-sheets

On the balcony
The bed-sheets were dripping
With the dew of a fragmentary dream—

The sun broke the layers of cloud
As the sheets became lighter in flapping
Making a slide-show—

The moon last night
Was tossing and turning in the bed of village wilderness
Covered with vegetable flowers   and green grass—

Don't know whose bride
Got up early
And washed her sheets by stealth

姐姐的紫云英

你盛开的紫云英
浪涛似地一波波涌来
把我推到了天边

我无处立足
被你的浪漫卷走——

在你汹涌的折腾中
在你美丽的燃烧中
我呼喊：
姐姐，姐姐！

My sister's milkvetch

Your milkvetch in full bloom
Came surging, like waves
Pushing me to the edge of the sky

I couldn't get a foothold
Carried away by your romance—

In your surging zhetenging
In your beautiful burning
I cried out loud:
Sister, sister!

尼采档案馆

尼采的红墙房
坐落在魏马
坡

精神失常的
尼采
冬天不开
门

我上了坡
只能隔着铁门
看一簇簇
白雪果
伸出栅栏 在
风中 凋
零

The Archives of Nietzsche

The red-walled house
Is situated on a slope
In Weimar

The mental
Nietzsche
Never opened his door
In winter

When I climbed up the slope
I could only see through the iron door
Clusters
Of white-snow fruit
Extending across the fence   withering
In the
Wind[4]

---

4 Note that this is a found poem, based on a paragraph from an article by Zhang
Lushi, in *News China*, published on 15/01/2018.

拔毛

4 月 9 日
北京动物园
一只熊猫
趴在木架上睡觉
悄悄飞来一只乌鸦
在它背上拔毛

乌鸦用满嘴的白毛
在园外的树上
做窝

我想
这样的老鸦窝
准是国宝级
别

乌鸦
一次次飞来又飞走
熊猫
一直没醒来

Removing the hair

On the 9th April
In the Beijing Zoo
A panda was asleep, on its stomach
When a magpie came flying over
To remove its hair on its back

The magpie, its beak filled with white hair
Used it to make a nest
In a tree outside the zoo

I thought such a magpie nest
Must be a living
Treasure of the
Nation

The magpie
Came and went
But the panda
Never woke up[5]

---

5 Note that this is a found poem, based on *News China*, No. 14, 2018.

男人

爬不动了还爬
爬上去了还爬
男人就想爬

上不去要上
上去了还想上

一上一上又一上
一上上到山头上
山头上的男人
就那副
熊样！

一下一下又一下
一下下到山底下
山底下的男人
又一副
熊样！

Men

Trying to climb even when they can't
Trying to climb further even when they reach the top
Men do like climbing

They want to get up when they can't
They still want to get up when they can

Getting up, up and up
Right up to the top of the mountain
But the men on top
Look so
Boring!

Then they get down, down and down
Till they reach the bottom
The men at the bottom of the mountain
Still look so
Boring!

火车客栈

一列不知从哪里
开来的火车
停在 P
镇
常有旅客
上车
下车

背包客　驴友
流浪者
诗人
在车厢里
聊天　喝酒　撒尿
睡觉——

列车
在风雪中呼啸了一夜
仍在那个站头

The train inn

A train
from nowhere
is parked at Town
P
often there are passengers
who go on board it
or off it

backpackers   travel pals
bums
poets
in the compartments
they chat   drink   piss
or sleep—

the train
kept roaring all night in the wind and snow
but never left the station

一只旧包

扔在角落
想翻找点什么
把它翻了出来
拉开拉链
那破包
一拉就破了——

翻来找去
除了夹层里
一张某人的名片
一件破事也
找不到了

我撕了那张名片
突然想起点
什么

An old bag

Is discarded in a corner
When I wanted to find something
I found it
Unzipped it
But the broken bag
Broke up when unzipped—

I ransacked it
But could find nothing
Not even a broken thing
Except someone's name card
In the lining

I tore the card up
When suddenly I thought
Of something

找鞋

一个浪头
带走了一只拖鞋
小男孩哭了
旁边的大叔说
别哭
我帮你找回来

大叔把留在沙滩上的
那一只
放在水面
拖鞋打漂了一下
沉下去了

在沉鞋的地方
他找到了
另一半

Looking for the other slipper

A wave
Carried a slipper away
The little boy burst into tears
An uncle by his side said
Don't cry
I'll help you find it back

The uncle put the other slipper left
On the beach
On the water
The slipper
Turned around
Before it sank

And where it sank
He found the other
One

挂钟

挂了
从墙上拿下来
换了 5 号电也不动
挂了——
走碎步的那个女人死了
定格在 19:38 分
这个时辰
农历 2018.8.14 的
月亮
挂上了树梢

The hanging clock

Hanged dead

Taken down off the wall

It refused to move even after the batteries were replaced

Hanged dead—

The woman in mincing steps died

Fixed at 7.38pm

When, on 14 August 2018, on the Chinese calendar

The moon

Was hanging on a branch

雨的支票

劈里啪啦
账房先生打了一夜的算盘
一夜的如意算盘
粒粒进
粒粒是加法
稻谷　麦粒　豆子
粒粒是金子　银子　铜板
天上掉银子　金子
铜板
掉了一夜
噼里啪啦　噼里啪啦
噼里啪啦一夜
老板娘受不了啦　光脚
跑下楼梯
摔坏了粒粒皆辛苦的
算盘

The cheque of rain

Pilipala, pilipala
The accountant worked on his abacus all night
A night of wishful thinking by abacus
Adding up grain by grain
Every grain an addition
Rice   wheat   beans
Every grain is gold   silver
Copper coins
Dropping all night
Pilipala pilipala
Pilipala all night
His wife, no longer able to bear it all   ran barefoot
Downstairs
And smashed the abacus
Of all the hard grains

明月

明月几时
有？
把酒问青天
青天
阴着脸
你问谁去？

明明如月
何时可掇？
明月就在你头上
你摘得到么？

举杯邀明月
不如陪红颜
把酒
酒吧
与美人同醉
何以解忧
唯有浓睡

南京有雨
上海多云
南京的
月
在躲雨
上海的
月
泡在浴缸里

The bright moon

When do we have the bright
Moon?
Holding up the wine cup you ask the sky
But the sky
Has a dark face
Who do you ask?

Such a bright moon
But when can you take it down?
The bright moon over your head
But can you pluck it?

Inviting the bright moon with your cup
Is not as good as keeping company with a beautiful woman
Holding a wine cup
In a bar
And getting drunk with her
How do you get rid of all your concerns
Except by having a sound sleep?

There is rain in Nanjing
But Shanghai is overcast
While the moon
In Nanjing
Is dodging the rain
The moon
In Shanghai
Is getting soaked in a bath tub